I hope that my achievements in life shall be these - that I will have fought for what was right and fair, that I will have risked for that which mattered, and that I will have given help to those who were in need, and that I will have left the earth a better place for what I've done and who I've been. ~~~~Author C. Hoppe

"Do the right thing, even when no one is looking."

*"Admit when you are wrong, and battle when
you know you are right."*

"It is, what it is."

~Mottos of Darren Tolsma

This book is dedicated to my late husband Darren Tolsma. Darren was a devoted husband and father who loved his family, his God, and his country. Darren was my, and my children's, everything. He was on a business trip and just wanted to get home to his family, so he booked an early flight home, and on a cold wintery night on February 12, 2009; everything changed.

I will love you forever Darren, and you will never be forgotten.

This book is also dedicated to my children, Darren and Nicole, who have given me so much strength, encouragement, and support. I love them both so much, they will always be the greatest gifts I ever received from their father.

(Note: You will notice there is a larger than normal top margin on every page. I wanted my story to be read and the reader to experience my emptiness at the same time. The blank top margin represents my emptiness since Darren has been gone.)

Everything Changed

All Rights Reserved © 2012 by Robin Tolsma

Front Cover: Robin Tolsma

Back Cover: Robin Tolsma

Photo Credits: All photos were submitted by Robin Tolsma with the exception of those credited and used with permission by The White House, The Buffalo News, and Derek Gee.

Published by Robin Tolsma/LuLu Enterprises, Inc.

Printed in the United States of America

First Printing: March 2012

ISBN: 978-1-4583-8442-3

Everything Changed

Robin Tolsma

Everything Changed

It is really hard to write about the worst day of my life.
Three years later, I still don't believe any of this is true. I think it
is more that I don't want to believe it.   I think that I am living
someone else's nightmare and I will wake up, and my husband will
be snoring **LOUDLY** next to me, and my life will be normal once
again…but that won't happen. He's gone; dead.

I don't want to believe that Darren died in a plane crash.
Planes don't just fall out of the sky; well that's what I thought
before February 12, 2009. I know differently now.

My husband, Darren, was scheduled to come home from his
business trip around 10:30 p.m. the night of February 12th. He
called home from the New Jersey airport around 7:00 p.m. and
asked me to check the computer for earlier flights; I did. I told him

not to bother trying US Air flights; they were cancelled across the board. He said there was an earlier fight on Continental and he would be home about an hour earlier if he switched flights. He was excited because he would be able to see the kids before they went to bed for the night; he hated not seeing them. Darren booked Continental Flight 3407. He briefly spoke to our kids, Darren 19 and Nikki 16, at the time. The last thing he said to the kids, and to me was, "I love you." Those were the last words he would ever speak to any of us…ever.

The night of February 12, 2009 was a normal night at home for Darren (D), Nikki, and me, as we waited for my husband, their dad, to come home. It was a cold night; that I remember. It had snowed the night before and during the day. I was a teacher then, and I had hoped for a snow day. The roads were icy, the wind whipped around. Darren would have said, "t'is not a fit night out for man nor beast." He said that a lot on cold days. Darren was a hopeless romantic and loved those holiday classics; that was from

Rudolph the Red Nosed Reindeer; he loved those shows. On this particular night, it was not a good night to be outside or to be flying. The kids and I sat in the living room with the fireplace on. Nikki had a broken leg and was lying on the couch. D, all six feet of him, was curled up on the small love seat, yielding the couch to his injured sister. He was always doing things like that; so much like his dad…always polite, always kind, always thinking of others first. Nikki was being… well… Nikki. She was holding steadfast to being the reason I color my hair; she was taking advantage of her injury and was comfortably sprawled out on the couch.

I remember the three of us were watching America's Best Dance Crew on MTV. Nikki wanted to check the computer to see how long before Dad's flight landed. I walked behind her as she hopped into the office, crutches apparently were too cumbersome, so she often hopped on her good leg. Nikki and I watched together as the computer screen showed that flight 3407 had landed. It was 10:17 p.m., and then the screen went blank. It would be about 20 or 25 minutes before Darren got home from the airport and our "mad dash clean-up" began. My husband was a neat freak, of sorts, so we always wanted the house to look its best when he walked in the door. After the quick tidying, Nikki and D resumed their respective couches. I decided to go lay down in the sitting room, in the front of the house, so I would hear Darren when he arrived home from his trip. We all fell asleep.

I woke up at 1:40 a.m. and walked into the living room, both kids were sound asleep. I remember waking them and asking if anyone had heard from Dad, they said, "No." So I figured Darren had gone up to work to drop off his briefcase before coming home. I turned off the TV, told the kids to go up to bed, and I followed. I tried my husband's cell phone; it went immediately to voicemail. I assumed he had forgotten to turn it on and that he was up at work. I tried his phone every 30 minutes after that. I remember being mad that he didn't turn his phone on. I called his work Blackberry; no answer. I called the office; no answer. I called his cell; no answer. I started to get upset. At least turn your phone on, I thought. I fell asleep, briefly, and in that short time, I had a dream that Darren had died and his funeral was at Queen of Heaven Church, where we got married. I woke up at 4:20 a.m. in a cold sweat. My cell phone was lit up. "Good," I said out loud, he finally left me a message, but it was not from him. It was from a track coach who simply texted, "Are you awake? Are you ok?" Why would the track coach send me that? Then I got that sick feeling in the pit of my stomach. I sat up in bed, grabbed my remote, turned on the TV, and read, in horror, that Continental Flight 3407 had crashed in Clarence Center. At that moment, a part of me died, and at that moment...*everything changed.*

I immediately went to my son's room. I said, "D! Please come in my room, I think Dad's plane crashed!" I remember I was so nervous and scared that I had a hard time speaking. D bolted out of bed came in my room, saw the image on the TV and yelled, "NO, NO, NO!" Seconds later, Nikki hopped into my room and saw D and I crying, looked at the TV and said, "Oh God no!" Her

crying was instant, she dropped to the floor and we were frozen,

numb, in shock, and in my bedroom at 4:35 a.m. on Friday,

February 13, 2009. The nightmare had begun.

The crawler on the bottom of the TV said, "Continental

Flight 3407 crashed in Clarence Center, 49 on board dead, one on

the ground." In our hysterics and shock, we assumed that one

person was alive on the ground. Nikki wanted to go to the crash

site immediately. She said, "If anyone could survive a plane crash

Mom, it's Dad." She knew Darren was always aware of the

aircraft he was on. He counted the rows of seats to the nearest

exits, always. He taught the kids how to do that when we traveled

too. "We have to go Mom," she said. We started to get dressed

but the news quickly confirmed our worst fear. There was one

person on the ground that was killed as well. There were "no

survivors" aboard the aircraft; none.

To this day, the sound of my and Darren's children's cries

haunt me. It was a sound I will never forget. It was the sound of pure pain. Nothing, and I mean nothing, I could do, would ever be able to take their pain away. I wanted to take all their pain…all of it; but I couldn't. We hugged each other, sat on my bed, and cried.

I had to call my parents. My dad couldn't understand me; he put my mom on the phone. They didn't even know Darren was out of town. I didn't bother telling anyone because it was such a short trip. *Darren left on February 10ᵗʰ early in the morning. I will never forget that morning. Darren fumbled in the dark to get ready. He didn't want to wake me up that early and when he tried to kiss me goodbye, his night vision wasn't so great, because he kissed my eyelid then found my forehead, then my lips. "Goodbye Rob, I love you," he said. I heard him whisper "I love you D, I love you Nick," as he walked down the stairs in the dark of the morning. He always did that when he left before the kids got up; always.* My parents, in shock, said they would come right over.

My second phone call was maybe the hardest phone call I would ever have to make in my life. I had to call Darren's parents. His mom answered the phone. She knew something was wrong because of the time, it was before 5:00 a.m., and no phone call is ever good at that time. I had to tell my mother-in-law that her son had died in a plane crash and that I didn't have any other information. She was confused and hung up. Within minutes, my father-in-law called back and I had to repeat what I knew; which was not much. He seemed much calmer and asked me to let him know when I found out for sure; he hung up too. My third call was to my department chair. *I was a seventh grade English teacher in the same town in which I live. I graduated, with honors in 2005 with my Bachelor's degree. With the encouragement of my husband and kids, I graduated with honors with my Master's in English in 2007. My teaching job in Lancaster, NY was a dream come true; a perfect job. I had been teaching there for five years and this was my tenure year.* I had to call work, but I honestly don't remember what I said now. I called my co-worker, Rita, who was my best friend at work, and then I called Joe and Sharon Downie. Joe worked with Darren, and he was like a brother to him. Then, I dropped my phone, walked into my bathroom, fell to my knees and begged the Lord to help me. "God, please, *PLEASE*, help me. I don't know what to do here. I don't know what I'm supposed to do. I don't know how to help my kids. Please help me help them." Then, I sobbed, silently, into a towel; I didn't want the kids to hear my pain, grief, or sadness.

I walked out of my bathroom, told the kids to get dressed and then I texted Dave Hall. Dave, then 19, was a family friend and a great friend to Nikki. My text said, "Darren's plane crashed. He is dead. Nikki needs you. Can you come over?" Dave was at our house in 17 minutes. He sat on the couch with Nikki, as she stared at the TV, and he held her. He rubbed her hair, her shoulders; he told her he was there for her. Thank God for Dave; he never left her side that day. *Dave left for the military two weeks later and he is dearly missed by the three of us. I call him my "Navy Dave"*

now; he will always be a special part of our lives.

D was pacing, we didn't know what to do. My parents came over about 30 minutes after I called them. I remember not wanting to cry but as soon as my dad and mom hugged me, the tears flowed uncontrollably. Rita soon followed my parents, she brought bagels and coffee. I did not want to eat, none of us did... for several days.

People started filing into my house the morning of Friday, February 13th. Truth be told, I didn't want to see any of them, but I didn't want to be alone either. I didn't know what I was supposed to do or say and I certainly didn't want to break down in front of my kids...and they kept coming; neighbors, friends, relatives, Darren's co-workers, my co-workers, and the track team. *Darren loved the track team. He knew everyone's stats, he encouraged every athlete to do their best, and he never missed one track meet. He even drove alone up to Dartmouth, Vermont to watch Nikki compete because I was home with pneumonia and he didn't want*

to miss seeing her run. Darren loved watching Nikki and D run.
Nikki was a sprinter and D was a distance runner. Darren just
loved to watch his kids compete. He also loved everything about
that team, the kids, the coaches, the parents. Darren knew the
stats of athletes from other school districts and he quickly made
friends with parents from all over Western New York. Everyone
involved with indoor and outdoor track loved Darren and he loved
them. Thank God for the track team, they were there to support and
comfort Nikki and D, and they distracted me from thinking, *my*
husband is dead. They cried with me and for me. They will never
know how much they meant to me during that time. And still, they
kept coming….people were everywhere and anywhere they could
find a place to sit in my house. They brought food and flowers,
sobbed, and cried. I tried to console them but after a while, I
wanted to disappear with my kids, somewhere, and just hold them
but that never happened.

D had gone up to UB by noon that day, he had an exam to

take, my dad offered to go with him, but he wanted to go alone. D

took the test and aced it, and wound up with a 4.0 GPA that

semester. I honestly don't know how he did it. I remember when I

asked him why he went to UB that day to take the test, he simply

said, "Dad would have wanted me to." He was right; Darren

would have.

Nikki went up to school that day too, to get her books. Dave

carried her; literally. Nikki also went to watch the track team

practice that day. She said she needed to do something normal and

that there were too many people in our house crying. The track

team distracted Nikki from the nightmare.

My kids, my father, my in-laws, and I had to go to the Indigo

Hotel, while my mother held down the fort at home for me. Mom

fed people she didn't know, and took message after message for

me; and she was so much more than my mom when I needed her.

It was at the Indigo Hotel that we were going to be briefed on what

happened. What did happen? How did this happen? Why did this happen? My biggest fear was the kids; God, help me help my kids.

I remember how my cheeks stung each time a tear rolled down, I had been crying non-stop since I woke up. My eyes were red, my cheeks burned, my head hurt, and my heart was shattered. I remember pulling up to the Indigo Hotel and I remember not knowing what to do.

We were told we had to get ID badges to enter the hotel. While we were being "processed," I can remember looking around and seeing grief and pain everywhere. I didn't want to be there and I certainly didn't want my kids to be there. The National Transportation Safety Board (NTSB) was giving a briefing in 30 minutes. I needed to find Jennifer West. *I had met Jennifer at a Northrop Grumman "after holiday" party eleven days earlier. Ironically, we even sat at the same table.* Jen had to be here, her husband was on that plane too. I walked into a small conference room and amid the sea of people....there she was. I started walking across the room and Jennifer spotted me and stood up, but that was so surreal. It seemed as though the room and everyone in it froze, except for Jen and I. It seemed as though we were moving in slow motion. We met halfway across the room, hugged, no…grabbed onto each other…and sobbed. That was the beginning of my lifelong connection with Jennifer West.

I remember how devastated Jen looked, and I remember how we asked each other if this was really happening. We both knew it was, but neither of us wanted to admit it. The NTSB briefing was about to begin, so we all walked into a very large and very crowded conference room and we listened, in silence, as Chairmember Cheelander, lead investigator for the NTSB, began to fill in the gaps of our nightmare. I sat with my kids, my dad, and my in-laws as the facts were presented to us. At one point, I saw Jennifer get up and run out of the room crying. I didn't see or talk to her for days after that. I remember hearing words and phrases I never wanted to hear, "co-mingling, frozen, dead on impact, charred, remains, and pieces." How on earth could I shield my kids from this? At the end of the briefing, my kids, dad, and I sat down with the chief medical examiner, Dr. Mark LeVaughn. He was a very compassionate man who took down notes about Darren. I described Darren's wedding ring and the inscription; he wrote that down. I described Darren's surgeries; he wrote that down. I described, in detail, the unique buckle on Darren's belt; he wrote that down. I described the color of Darren's eyes and hair; Dr. LeVaughn stopped writing. I remember looking Dr. LeVaughn in the eye and saying, "That's not going to matter anymore is it?" His response was simple, "I'm sorry." I froze inside and prayed that Darren did not suffer in his final moments; that is a fear I live with every day.

The drive home from the Indigo Hotel was silent. Dr. LeVaughn's and Member Cheelander's words echoed so loud in my mind. Please let this be a dream….please God! However, we didn't go straight home that night. We had to go to the airport and find my husband's car, brush off the snow, and bring it home. We knew Darren so well that it didn't take long before we found his car. My son insisted on driving it home…alone. He brushed off the snow, scraped the windows and brought his dad's car home. Tears ran down my cheeks as I followed my son, in his dad's car, on a bitterly cold night. My heart broke for D as he sat among his dad's possessions, in his dad's car, that would never be driven by his father again.

Everything changed. Walking into my house that night was eerie. I no longer felt safe, I no longer felt secure, and I no longer felt confident. I felt lost, scared, and abandoned. There were still people everywhere in my house and the food and flowers were non-stop. Neither the kids, nor I, could eat. Our lives where turned upside down, inside out, and backwards now; food was the last thing any of us wanted.

Nikki slept with me that night, although I wouldn't call what we did sleeping. *Nikki would often sleep with me when*

Darren went out of town. We would fall asleep in my bed with the TV on and snuggle. It was several months before Nikki would sleep in her own room again. I remember the first night she did; she was having a sleepover and I did not want to be alone in my room; I still don't. I was afraid of every noise and every sound in the house. Truth be told; I still am. I knew it was now my job to protect the kids and sleep wouldn't come for days. I still get chills, and tears, when I think of my son crying in his bathroom. My guys were best friends and my son was hurting. His pain still lingers in my ears and mind. Nikki turned to stone, her laughter, her smile...gone. I wanted to take all their pain away; all of it. I knew I couldn't and it killed me, it still does.

Darren and D had this unique father-son bond. They would often take late night walks that lasted hours. They always walked in the door giggling or smiling. Darren loved those late night walks with his son, and D loved them too; D has the memories now.

Darren drove Nikki to school every single morning. That was their father-daughter time. Darren often helped Nikki with her homework too. He loved spending time with his kids and he often resented the amount of time that Northrop Grumman demanded of him. Yet, he never made his kids feel second to work. He made time for all of us; always.

The only silent moments in our house, in the days following the crash, were during the hours of 4:00 am and 8:00 am. That's when I went through the mail and that's when I cried. I had no idea what to do, what bill to pay, how to pay a bill….that was Darren's job. My house was constantly packed with friends, family, and neighbors. Yet, I had never felt so alone and lost.

Continental flew my brother Ron, his wife Jennifer, and my niece Bobbi-Ann up to Buffalo. I remember being in shock for most of the time they were here, but glad they were. I needed Ron. He could always make me smile; so I thought… not this time.

The next few days were anything but routine, there were

two NTSB briefings a day at the Indigo Hotel. False reports had surfaced about the number of bodies recovered and the details were always heartbreaking. The kids and I had to give DNA samples, or swabs of our cheeks, for identification purposes. I remember how angry I was that my kids had to do this. No child should have to do this and certainly not mine; this was unfair to them; to anyone. God please help us.

My brother Darren, yes I do have a brother with the same name, had quickly become my rock. Mom still held down the fort for me at home while my dad, brother, kids, and I went to the Indigo Hotel every night hoping for some detail that would ease our horrific pain. Brother Darren and my dad took notes for me; I was incapable of tying my shoes at one point.

On February 17th, five days after the crash, at 9:30 p.m. I received 'the call.' Dr. Mark LeVaughn told me that Darren had been positively identified and that his body would be ready to be released to the funeral home. Dr. LeVaughn had a kind and soft voice and he spoke with compassion as he told me Darren was the first body identified, and that he was approximately 90% intact. He then asked me if I wanted to be notified if they found, and identified, the rest of Darren's remains. "Of course," I said. I did ask how Darren was identified. Dr. LeVaughn said, "By his fingerprints, his dental records, and the inscription on his wedding ring." *(Forever 8-29-86)* Joe and Sharon Downie were sitting with me when that call came through. We were up in Nikki's bedroom because it was the only place where we could plan Darren's memorial service and the only place that was quiet in my house. My son was doing his homework in my bedroom, he needed quiet too. I thanked Dr. LeVaughn, hung up the phone and then called Pacer Funeral Home. I realized, then, that this was real and I had to tell the kids; but how? Joe and Sharon hugged me; I fought back tears and was so thankful they were with me. I would have crumbled without them; I wonder if they know that?

D and Nikki sat and listened quietly as I, calmly, repeated

what Dr. LeVaughn had told me. D decided, at that point, that he wanted to speak at his dad's memorial service, Nikki couldn't do it; but we planned everything together.

Nikki went with me to pick out a place at Forest Lawn for Darren to be laid to rest. Dave Hall (Navy Dave) came with us that day. He stayed next to Nikki and he was able to make us both smile. I remember walking out of the cemetery's office and there was Dave; dancing outside, next to my car. I smiled for the first time in days. I chose the Serenity Mausoleum for Darren, it is beautiful there and I wanted him to be somewhere beautiful; like him.

The funeral home was incredibly hard for me. Todd Pacer, funeral director, was so compassionate. However, picking out the *last* of everything for Darren was heartbreaking for me. Todd was helpful, I wonder if he even knew how lost I was? Casket, urn, prayer cards, photo CD, music, obituary; it was all too much. I hated that I had to make choices; last choices. Todd guided me through everything and when I was about to cry, he let me. Todd is now a good friend of mine; I will never forget his compassion; ever. Todd was Jennifer's funeral director too, and the three of us are very good friends now.

Going to the crash site, days after the accident, was tough. The family members were loaded onto coach buses and driven out. It was odd because there was such media frenzy outside the Indigo Hotel that the grief stricken family members were not only escorted to the buses, by NTSB officials, but I remember that we were shielded by enormous golf umbrellas to hide our grief from the media. There, at the crash site, the smell of jet fuel was evident. I brought flowers and laid them down on the ground, I picked up a rock and put it in my pocket and said to myself, "This is where God came and took Darren home." I did not cry there, others sobbed, others wept, and some collapsed. I read a statement to the first (and last) responders and I remember holding onto my brother Darren's hand on one side and my cousin's on the other;

not wanting to let go. My cousin, Mike Bielanin, was, and still is, a Transit Authority police officer who was on duty, at the crash site, from the night the crash happened. He assured me, each night, that the bodies were not left unattended. I found that to be extremely comforting. Mike was at the crash site when I stepped off the bus and right into his arms. His comfort and compassion holds a special place in my heart; even today. My children did not go to the site that day. That was a sad day. My kids never stepped foot into the Indigo Hotel again either, the memories of that place were too painful, too sad, too horrible. I stopped going to the NTSB briefings after this day; I had Darren and the facts would take months to come out.

Northrop Grumman had sent a security guard to be at our house from 8:00 am until 8:00 pm. I personally wanted him there from night to morning because I was so afraid to be home at night, but I was grateful that someone was watching out for us at all. The media was relentless. The kids and I agreed to do an interview with the NBC Nightly News, and that was a decision that I regret; both my kids broke down. I remember D saying that his father was his best friend, and Nikki just sobbed. Our hearts were so broken and I didn't know how to fix them; everything changed....for all of us.

I hated the day, four days after the crash, in which the Northrop Grumman executives came by my house to offer their condolences. Three limousines showed up in front of my house and I remember that I felt that if I didn't let them in, none of this really happened. I didn't want to hear their condolences or their offers for help; I wanted my husband back and that they couldn't do!

We decided, days after the crash, that Darren's memorial service could only be held at the Lancaster High School's auditorium. After all, it was Darren's favorite place away from home. It was there, at the high school, that Darren watched our children soar. He watched them achieve. He watched them grow.

Darren was also such a huge supporter of the Lancaster High School track team and everyone on the team loved him, so it seemed only fitting to have the service at the high school.

I, however, *had* to plan everything. Darren's memorial service had to be perfect, and it had to be done completely by me. From the program, slide show, music and flowers, I planned and directed it all. I even MC'd the service. I had to; for Darren.

The day of the service was a cold, blustery, snowy, windy winter day. The high school auditorium was packed, over 1,100 people were in attendance. I had asked, in Darren's death notice, that only close family, friends and my current students attend, but Darren was loved by so many that they came….and came…and came. It was standing room only and a special overflow room had been opened in the gymnasium, which could only broadcast the audio of the memorial service.

Choosing the speakers for Darren's memorial service was easy. Me, my son D, my brothers Darren and Ron, my brother-in-law Jim, two boys from the track team; Ryan Woodard and Josh Mertzloft, and from Northrop Grumman; Joe Downie, Larry Robinson, and Ed Eberl but it was the last speaker, Coach Kevin Carriero that brought the house down and made me sob. *Darren had the utmost respect for our children's track coach. Darren and Kevin had a unique parent/coach bond that, by all accounts, was a very blessed friendship.*

The entire day of Darren's memorial service is still a bit fuzzy. The service was taped and, to this day, it is very hard for me to watch. I have yet to watch the entire service; it breaks my heart. It still doesn't seem real, and when I watch myself in the video I still feel like I am watching someone else "play" me. The funeral breakfast is a blur too. I do remember hearing that Dan Pappa, from Northrop Grumman, would be at the memorial service and the breakfast. I needed to find him and talk to him. I had never met him before; but I needed to…badly. *Dan was supposed to be on Flight 3407 the night of the accident. Dan worked with Darren and he was on the business trip with the other four co-workers in*

New Jersey. He drove the four men, from Northrop Grumman, to

the airport on February 12th. Instead of flying home that night

with them, Dan went to visit his parents in New Jersey. Dan was

given a second chance at life. I wanted to tell him that God had big

plans for him and I wanted to see what they were. I was so glad

that Dan, then 26, was not on that plane that night. We hugged

each other that day and Dan and I became lifelong friends. I even

consider Dan family. In fact, Dan calls me Aunt Robin, and I am

blessed by our friendship.

The kids and I decided that Darren needed an escort to

Forest Lawn Cemetery where he would be cremated. The entire

track team and both my and Darren's family followed the hearse.

There were over twenty cars in the procession. I drove the hearse; I

had to. I needed to give Darren his final ride and Todd Pacer let

me drive. Todd knew that I used to drive limousines and that I was

licensed to drive the hearse. I remember he said, "Are you sure you can do this?" Without hesitation I said, "Yes." Todd wanted to line up the cars and he said he wanted to give me a moment with Darren. I remember saying, "That's not Darren back there." Yet, when Todd shut the door, I turned around and said, "Darren, I am so sorry. I love you so much!" and I cried. When Todd came back into the passenger seat, I put on my game face. I still wear that face. It isn't often that anyone will see me cry or break down. I do that in private moments; alone.

The drive to Forest Lawn went by too quickly. I wanted to drive that hearse forever and never stop. Todd had asked the kids, and me, if we wanted to put any items in the casket with Darren when he was cremated; we did. Darren gave his father his sneakers that he ran a full marathon in. Nikki gave her father her track spikes that she won so many races in. I gave my honors tassels to Darren because he was so proud of me for graduating college with honors; he was my biggest source of support. Other family members left notes and letters too. I remember kissing my hand and placing it on Darren's oak casket and saying 'I love you Darren." The kids followed suit, and the ride home was quiet and somber and reflective.

When D, Nikki and I got home from the cemetery, it was the first time, in days, that our house was empty, but 'we' were empty too. Nine days after the crash and the three of us were alone. We talked that day about how all decisions, from that point forward, would be made by the three of us and how we would all have to pitch in to run this house as efficiently as Darren did. D was now the man of the house and my heart broke for him. Nikki lost her sense of security and her pain was so buried; she forgot how to smile for a while. I was strong on the outside but a mess on this inside. I would not tell anyone how I felt, I often said, "I'm fine," and I still do. It really means I am far from fine but don't want anyone to know. I needed to handle everything by myself and I needed to prove, to my husband, that he set an example that was easy for me to follow on running a household and raising kids;

it was not easy though. I had no idea what I was doing; I still feel lost and I feel so guilty.

Two days after the memorial service, and the escort to Forest Lawn, we were once again headed right back to the cemetery. Eleven days after the crash, we had a very private internment service for Darren conducted by Rev. Thomas Quinlivan (Queen of Heaven). My family and Darren's family were there; it was devastatingly sad. My son carried his dad's urn and placed it in the niche' in the Serenity Mausoleum. My heart broke for my children. I wanted to scream, I wanted to weep, I wanted to punch something, but I remained stone-cold still and let only a few tears roll down my cheeks. I kissed the urn, placed a photo of my husband and a stopwatch in the niche' with him, and made the silent ride home with my family.

Two days after Darren's memorial service, Nikki came down with mono. I remember how sick she was. I panicked and begged the Lord not to take her too. She was weak, frail, sick and hurting. I felt helpless. D became quiet, Nikki didn't speak much and I hated the way our lives had changed, I hated the way everything changed.

Our personal grieving couldn't begin yet. There was still Ernie West's memorial service and the Northrop Grumman service for the four Northrop men who died on the plane too. I broke down at Ernie's service. I sat next to Joe Downie and I sobbed. I sat next to Joe at the Northrop Grumman service too. That was somber. Although Northrop celebrated each of the four lives lost, the photos and music were painful reminders of their absence. Trying to be strong for Darren's co-workers was a challenge; but I did it.

Joe Downie was a huge help during the days, weeks, and months following the crash. Joe helped me solicit an attorney, Hugh Russ, and Joe and his wife Sharon, have supported me through every step of this nightmare. Joe helped me sort out papers, my finances (I knew nothing about that stuff), get my taxes ready, and both he and his wife offered a shoulder when I needed one.

I had taken a leave of absence from my teaching job. I loved my job. I used to brag about my students to Darren all the time. My students were the reason I left my house with a smile on my face and why I came home with one. Now, I knew I wasn't what was good for the students anymore. My heart was broken, my life shattered, and I had to figure out how to live without Darren. "God, help me,' was what I would find myself saying so many times in a day. After being married for 23 years and meeting Darren on a blind date when I was 17, I was lost. I had a security system put in my house and blinds put on all my windows almost immediately; I was afraid all the time. Truth be told, I am still afraid. I am still uncomfortable in my own house because everything changed.

I met Darren on a blind date on January 2, 1983. I was 17 and Darren was 19. My cousin and Darren's friend were dating and they thought the two of us should meet. For me, it was love at first sight. Nothing else in my life mattered as much as Darren did. From that day forward, I hated our time apart and loved our time together. We got married three and a half years later and I was living a fairy tale, but then, on a cold winter night in February; everything changed.

I decided early on that I wanted to band together with the other 3407 family members and fight to make changes in Washington, DC so that this nightmare would never happen again. Aviation safety became not only a priority, but something I needed to do so my husband's death would not be in vain. I also knew that I wanted to fight Colgan, Continental, and Bombardier to make certain that they were properly punished. These issues became my mission, my goal, my desire, and my purpose.

D, Nikki and I made one of the first trips down to Washington, DC in May of 2009 to help lobby for aviation safety. Nikki spent her 17th birthday in an aviation subcommittee room and met numerous Senators and Congressman. We met with the head of the FAA too. My children pounded the pavement with me in DC; out of respect and honor for their father. I couldn't have been more proud of them. The 3407 family members had a very long road to climb; changing legislation would not be an easy task.

Shortly after we got home from Washington, DC in May, I received another call from Dr. Mark LeVaughn, the medical examiner. He told me that another 'piece' of Darren was positively identified and he wanted to know if I wanted to claim 'the remain' and have it cremated as well. Of course I did. I remember asking if he was calling Jennifer West, he was. I asked if I could break the news to her, or if at the very least he could wait until I got to her house to call her. I wanted to be there with her when the call came through. Jennifer was having a rough time; so was I. I knew how she felt and vice versa. First, I needed to tell my children what Dr. LeVaughn had just told me.

I remember sitting on my front porch and wondering, how

on earth was I going to tell the kids that there was another 'piece' of their father that had been positively identified? Telling them was awful, but their decision was simple, the kids wanted me to claim 'the remain.' That meant another trip to Pacer Funeral Home was on my schedule. Jennifer and I both received almost the exact same remains back. The cruelness of this was that in New York State you have to have a "container" to have any remains cremated. So, Jennifer and I had to pick out small caskets and go through then entire burial process once again; it was heartbreaking.

Jennifer and I had unanswered questions about our husbands. Together we went to the medical examiner's office. There, we spent four hours talking to Dr. Mark LeVaughn about our husbands' deaths. Dr. LeVaughn assured us that all the passengers and crew died on impact. He told us about the extensive trauma to both Darren and Ernie; but that information wasn't enough. Jennifer and I wanted… no needed, to see their autopsy photos. Dr. LeVaughn spent a long time trying to convince us that seeing an autopsy photo would be a mistake. For me, he was right, seeing Darren's photo was a mistake. I know why I needed to see the photo of my husband; my mind still didn't believe that Darren was dead. I suppose I thought that if I saw his body, it would have the same effect on me as going to his wake. I would finally believe he was gone; WRONG. The photo wasn't even recognizable as being a human. If not for Darren's shoe, I would not have known if I was looking at Darren or a bear, and his photo haunts me to this day. My nightmares often include this image. Yes, nightmares; more like night terrors. I wake up screaming multiple times in a week. My daughter has asked me when the nightmares will end, I wish I knew.

Four months after the crash, both Jennifer and I received our letters, that the "associated" items, or in other words "Darren and Ernie's personal possessions" were identified. We would be able to view them on a website and claim the items if we wanted them. Once again, our hearts were ripped open. It was on this website that I found Darren's wedding ring, clothing fragments, his laptop, and his torn shoe. I remember crying when I saw his "things" on the computer screen. I only recognized the ring and his shoe, and the pain in my heart surfaced once again. God help me.

I checked off the items I knew to be Darren's, and I sent my form back to Global BMS, the company who was taking care of all the personal effects. I remember that Jennifer had such a long list of Ernie's belongings and I had a very short one. I am not sure why, but this opened up so many questions. Did Darren check his baggage? Where was Darren's wallet? Were Darren and Ernie really seated next to each other? It would be weeks before I would get these items back, but there was only one item I wanted; the ring.

I don't think I will ever forget the day I received Darren's ring. Jennifer and I let a local camera crew (WIVB) film the two of us receiving our husband's personal effects; it was one of the few times I cried on camera. Darren's ring was the first item that was handed to me. What I remember most, was how kind and compassionate the people from Global BMS were, and how each individual item was wrapped in tissue paper; as if it where the most precious gift in the world. I also remember the smell. It smelled like jet fuel and smoke and although Global cleaned everything, the smell was so strong. Jennifer and I thought it smelled like death.

Darren's ring was handed to me in a small black velvet box. I opened it and I cried. The inscription "Forever 8-29-86" was visible and I slipped the 2mm gold wedding band on my finger and cried. *The last time I held that ring in my hand, I put it on Darren's finger; on our wedding day.* I also received his Bostonian black leather shoe, it was sliced in half. The black nylon sock they gave me was also cut down the middle; perfectly matching the shoe. I cradled that shoe to my chest and thought of the terror Darren must have experienced. Then, I put both the shoe and sock back in the box, covered it with the tissue paper and moved on to the four small pieces of clothing; fragments were what they were really. I received a five-inch square, tattered and ripped, piece of his once white dress shirt, a piece of the waist band of his pants and a small piece of his underwear. Darren's laptop was smashed, but intact, and it had that horrid smell of death that Jennifer and I had grown to hate. I buried everything, but the laptop and ring, in my yard. I gave the laptop back to Northrop Grumman and the ring is either on my finger or locked safely away. Jennifer, I remember, got a lot of Ernie's personal effects back, his wallet, pictures of their daughter Summer, his suitcase (albeit empty), but she did not get Ernie's wedding ring and my heart broke for her.

Continuing on with daily life has not been easy. I never realized, well, maybe it is I never fully understood how much Darren did for me and the kids. I feel terrible now that I had taken all of that for granted. Darren did the bill paying, laundry, cleaning, most of the cooking, the grocery shopping, the shoveling, all the outside work; what on earth did I do? Now, every single responsibility was left to me and on top of running a house and raising the kids alone, I wanted to take down the airline and get legislation changed. In short, I was taking on too much and crumbling on the inside; asking for help was not an option for me and so I had a 'lapse in judgment" (LIJ).

My LIJ is not something I am proud of, by any means, but for all the people who commented on how strong I was, and what a role model I was…I felt like a fake. On one particular day, when my kids were gone, I decided to put Jack Daniels in my coffee, just a shot at first to "relax" me. That shot soon became two, then three, and soon I saw no reason for coffee and drank over half a bottle of Jack Daniels by myself. I wanted to be with Darren that day and I decided that "Jack" and a razor blade could help me get to him. The Lancaster Police thought differently. I must have said, or texted, someone who sent help. I don't remember much after I hit the floor. Embarrassed; of course. Foolish; yes. Necessary to have a breakdown; yes. Was that the only time that happened; no. Will I do that again; no...or at least I hope not.

I guess, in part, I felt like I failed Darren. I didn't realize what he did for me and the kids on a daily basis, all the while working sixty, or more, hours a week. I didn't feel that I gave him the attention that he deserved. I do know that he knew I loved him, but I have guilt; lots of guilt. There was, and is, so much I wish I had said to him. So many wasted moments; gone. I do not do things even a fraction of how well Darren did them. I had even forgotten to open the mail, which I let pile up for weeks, and subsequently didn't open the bills (nor pay them) and my electric was shut off. I was embarrassed that I couldn't even keep up with the mail; how pathetic.

Nine months after the crash and my heart was once again torn apart. Jennifer and I received a very long list of "unassociated item," or items that were found among the wreckage from the crash. However, the ownership of these items was unknown. Basically, this was an itemized list of everything found at the crash site, and we had to go through the list (computer visual catalog) item by item, and try to find something/anything that may have belonged to our husbands. Jennifer and I did this together, and once again, we let the local TV news station (YNN) film this process. I remember hoping that Ernie's ring would on the list this time. We searched through over 40,000 items together. It was so sad to see belongings of the other passengers and from the family in the house that was hit. They were items that may have been worn or cherished, but items that belong to somebody. The only items I claimed and received were Darren's car fob and house key; nothing else. Jennifer found an eyeglass case that she had bought for Ernie, and on that last web page, we both knew that Ernie's ring was not there; together we wept.

My lawsuit against Colgan, Continental and Bombardier was underway, and I had to fill out a thirty page form and figure out the hours, per day, that Darren was: a tutor, mentor, cleaner, landscaper, confidant, counselor, shopper, gardener, etc. Were they kidding me?! Darren was a full time father to our kids. If they called his cell phone, he picked up. If they needed help with homework, he was available. Now I had to put an hour and dollar amount on the value of his time and everything he did? I hate you Colgan; hate you!

Jennifer and I received the "unassociated items" on Jennifer's 40th birthday; that I remember. The items were once again wrapped with care, and also accompanied by the smell of death. I remember that Jen and I hugged the Global BMS people for treating us so kindly and handling the items with such care.

I took Darren's house key off the broken key fob and I now carry his house key on my key ring. It's my daily reminder that he didn't make it home. I don't honestly need the key as a daily reminder. I live in the airport flight path and low flying planes are continual and constant; and my heart is empty. There is no mistaking the sound of a Dash 8-Q400, I call that sound, "the sound of death." Each time I see a plane, especially a Bombardier Dash 8-Q400 Colgan operated aircraft; I pray that it lands safely. Then my mind wonders to Darren...how scared was he?

I suppose most people would think it was bizarre that I got a *third* call from the medical examiner's office about Darren, but I didn't. There was going to be a third burial of the "unidentified" remains. I knew, based on the autopsy report, autopsy photo, and the second set of remains I got back, that a part of Darren was going to be buried in that grouping. So, another memorial service, another funeral, so to speak, and another burial. Nine months after the crash and I was still burying pieces of Darren. Once again, my and my children's hearts were broken. The service was also at Forest Lawn Cemetery and was mainly organized by the 3407 families and the Erie County Medical Examiner's office. It was beautiful. I had never seen such beautiful caskets in my life, or so many faces of sadness. My children, my family, and some of

Darren's Northrop Grumman friends were there for the final goodbye of sorts; it was another sad day. Continental had flown my brother Ron and his family up for the service. Having my family close by was important to me; I needed them. Ron was able to bring a smile to my face this time.

I hated the holidays that first year. I had spinal-fusion bone graft surgery and both my kids had dates, so we had distractions and support for the first Thanksgiving, Christmas, and New Year without Darren. I remember the hardest thing, for me, was wondering if I should put three or four stockings on the mantle. I decided four; just because Darren wasn't here, didn't mean he didn't love us. Somehow, we made it through. I spent, and still spend many nights crying in bed. My pillows are very familiar with my tears; even today.

In the weeks before the one year anniversary of the crash, I made, what I believe to be, the biggest mistake of my life. I had been made aware that a certain CD of the crash photos existed. I, in my desperate need to find closure, was bound and determined to find that disc; I did. In what I will regret for the rest of my life, was the decision to view the photos of my husband at the crash site. I will only say that closure was not what I found, nor was comfort. In fact, I inflicted upon myself heartache, grief, and pain of enormous magnitude. I can never erase these images from my mind, nor can I come to terms with what I saw. I will tell no one what I saw, or how it came to be that I viewed the photos. What I will tell you is that I wrecked myself that day, and I will never fully recover; ever. I will also tell you that I cannot look at a staked out lawn (the kind where someone has marked a gas or water lines with flags before they dig) the same way ever again. The photos had those same kinds of flags, but they didn't mark a utility, they marked a body. It makes me weep just thinking about it. The pain that brings to me is immense, and those flags represent a part of the image I saw. I made a mistake….a big one. The nightmares have been even more numerous and horrifying. I prolong sleeping as long as possible in hopes that I can thwart off the horror that plagues my mind. Yet, I also know that I would do that all over again. I would view the photos again because "I" needed to know. I often wonder why people call it 'closure.' There will really never be closure for me; ever. I feel as though Darren went missing and that everything that has happened has been someone else's story; someone else's nightmare; but it isn't....it's mine.

The one year anniversary of the crash was a solemn day for everyone. Jennifer and I had a "Light the Way Home" campaign going. We had asked that everyone turn their porch lights on during the hour from 10:00 -11:00 pm on February 12th. That was the hour our husbands would have come home. It signified two things; a way to remember the lives lost on Flight 3407, and it was our hope that everyone made it home safely, no matter what form of transportation they were using. I was overwhelmed by the number of porch lights on that night.

There was a memorial walk from the crash site to the airport on the one year anniversary. My back surgery was the reason I could not complete the 10 mile walk that the other 3407 family members did. I met everyone at the finish line, but that failed in comparison to walking in the freezing cold. I didn't go to the candlelight vigil that night either. I was actually scared that it would be too sad. The odd thing was that I had a ton of guilt over *not* going. I felt, once again, like a bad wife. My life is full of guilt now. One year and I still couldn't believe my husband was dead.

There seemed to be an endless sea of papers to sign and have notarized. The 'other' side wanted copies of Darren's medical records, dental records, high school, and college transcripts. Were they kidding me!? Darren was just a businessman who bought a plane ticket to come home. *HE* didn't cause this accident. Why do they need to know this information about him? Then it hit me, they were trying to come up with a dollar value of Darren's life, his net worth. Darren worked on a Combat Electromagnetic Environmental Warfare Simulator, he worked on programs for early detection of roadside bombs, he taught pilots how to use the equipment *HE* designed and now the other side wants a 'net worth' of his life; I hate you Colgan!

I spent a good portion of 2010 being a spokesperson and advocate for aviation safety, along with Jennifer West and the other 3407 family members. It was our goal, and still is, to let everyone know how poorly Colgan trains their pilots, what aloofness Continental has towards their subcontractors, and what disregard for safety Bombardier has for their aircraft. We also wanted to expose the FAA for their lack of implementing any of the NTSB's recommendations. At the time of the Flight 3407 crash, there were 26 unresolved recommendations to the FAA by the NTSB, there are now over 40. The FAA is neither pro-active nor re-active; they are in-active and the flying public needs to know that the FAA has a blatant disregard for aviation safety.

Jennifer and I made several trips to Washington, DC together. We were able to voice our concerns and demand change.

I met President Obama in May of 2010. He was making a scheduled trip to Buffalo and agreed to meet with ten of the family members from Flight 3407. I wore Darren's picture on my lapel and his ashes around my neck that day. When I told the President that Darren's ashes were in my locket, he hugged me. He promised to sign the bill when, and if, it came across his desk. I wanted to see the President have a more active role in aviation safety; he disappointed me.

In Washington, DC, Jennifer, I, and the other Flight 3407 family members personally met with numerous Senators and Congressmen/woman. We visited EVERY Senator's office, all the while carrying very large photos of our husbands. The photos were poster size and we were often asked if it was cumbersome to carry such large photos everywhere. It was easy because we did it for Darren and Ernie.

Jennifer and I got to speak our minds in Senator Corker's office, along with several other 3407 family members. He was holding up the Aviation Safety Bill. When we were done, the hold was lifted. We were elated! We were also there, with my son Darren, when the Senate and the House passed the Aviation Safety Bill HR5900; we wept that day too. President Obama signed the bill into law four days later. My parents were visiting me when the call came through that the bill was signed. We were ecstatic and immediately took flowers to the 3407 memorial sarcophagus at Forest Lawn and then went to see Darren; that was bittersweet.

My litigation, or mediation, began in June of 2010. I spent many sleepless nights researching previous regional airline crashes and gathering as much information on Colgan, Continental, and Bombardier as I could. I was in constant contact with Hugh Russ, my attorney, and I believe I may have even made a pest out of myself; too bad. I wanted justice. The day before my mediation, Jennifer and I did some TV news interviews, my message was clear, "Colgan, I'm coming for you." I meant it. Their negligence took away my husband, confidant, and best friend and they took my children's father, security, and support away. They messed with me, now it's my turn. LET ME AT THEM!

Mediation, June 17, 2010. I brought my brother Darren with me. I also brought along that daily edition of the Buffalo News. It had a story about Continental's CEO, in which he said, "I am not responsible for the safety of every flight." Armed with my newspaper, and the support of my brother, I was ready to face 'the others.' I'll never forget that day; ever. Four smartly dressed lawyers from the 'other' side, two of my attorneys, my brother, and I were in attendance. This would be the only day I would be allowed to speak to the 'other' side and say whatever I wanted. To the best of my knowledge and memory, this is what I said:

"You killed my husband. You took away my children's father. You took my security, safety, and love away from me and my kids. To you, Darren is just a case number, so let me tell you a

little about my husband. Darren and I met on a blind date on

January 2, 1983. It was love at first sight. Together we brought

two beautiful children into this world and together we could

handle anything. Darren did everything for us; the cooking, the

cleaning, grocery shopping, laundry, yard work; everything. He

never complained. He made a name for himself in the defense

contractor industry and he worked to save lives. In fact, he was

working on an aircraft survivability and surveillance program for

the military. He loved the military, loved his family, and his

country. Our troops were safer because of him; and you killed

him. You don't care. I brought in today's paper, which I am sure

you are aware of, but which justifies my line of thinking; you

screwed up! I loved my husband, and I have become a local

spokesperson for aviation safety, and you know what? I am good

at it. The public loves me, I want to make the air travel safer for

the public, and you people have left me with nothing but time on

my hands now. I now have time to research, time to be an activist,

time to make sure you never do this to anyone again! In the eyes
of the public, and especially here in Western New York, I am the
face of your mistake. So I am telling you, right here and right now,
do not insult me today, do not insult my children, and above all do
not insult my husband's memory." Then, I stopped talking and let
my attorney say a few words. We then went into separate rooms,
theirs and ours; and we waited. The 'other' side did insult me that
day. I cannot discuss my litigation but I became a very angry
widow. I had told the mediator that I wanted the 'others' to watch
my husband's four minute memorial service video. The mediator
assured me he would tell them to, but I insisted they watch
it...with me; they did.

It was hard to look at the video of my husband's smiling
face. All the months of pain, the burials, paperwork, and grief
caught up with me in that conference room at that moment, and I
wept. My brother, Darren, held me for support and strength and I
sobbed as person after person, in the video, spoke of Darren, spoke

of his character, and spoke of how much they loved him. The 'others' cried too. I thanked them for watching the video, walked back into 'our' room and cried on my brother's shoulder uncontrollably. Kyle Reeb, one of my attorneys cried too. He later told me he had no idea how I got through that day; me either. My brother Darren cried too. *Husband Darren and brother Darren were very close. My husband loved my brother as if he was his own brother and not just a brother-in-law. My husband loved my brother's wife Kelley so much too, and he adored the only nieces and nephew he knew; Gwen, Lydia, and Reid. The day we found out Darren had died, Gwen (our Godchild, who was seven at the time) walked into my house carrying the Christening photo of her with her Uncle Darren, tears streaming down her cheeks. Gwen still keeps that photo close to her.*

My litigation/negotiation lasted just shy of eight weeks. It was on August 13, 2010 that the 'other' side and I hit a wall. I either took their offer or I would go to trial. Sweet Jesus, I didn't want to go to trial. I didn't want my kids to have to testify or see or hear evidence that would cause further hurt or scars; and I settled. I called my financial advisor, Christopher Scott, before I accepted 'the other's' offer; in tears. We discussed amounts which would spread out into years and the value of a life. What made my decision a bit easier was a man I saw, while I was looking out the window, as I was speaking to Christopher on the phone. Across from the lawyer's office, sitting outside on a warm summer day, looking up to the sky was a man with severe cerebral palsy. I watched him as he smiled at each person that passed him by; some acknowledged him, some did not but yet…he smiled. I looked at this man and said to myself, "What would money do to change his life?" So, I asked my attorney if I could leave for a moment. I wanted to go sit next to this man and see what he saw; see why he was smiling; see why he was happy. My attorney wouldn't let me leave his office. Looking back, that was a good thing because I probably would have bolted home. I settled my lawsuit that day.

That part of my life was now over. No more fighting with a mediator, Colgan, Continental or Bombardier; it was over.

The second set of holidays, to me, was worse than the first. I remember dreading them, and I recall how much I missed Darren; I still do. Darren loved the holidays, he loved the way I decorated the house, and he loved shopping for me and the kids. It was so hard to put the ornaments on the tree the second Christmas. I did all the decorating that year alone; again. I tried very hard to make things easy for D and Nikki and I wasn't sure how *they* felt the second Christmas without their dad. So, I decorated alone and I cried...a lot. Putting the ornaments on the tree was especially hard because each one of our ornaments had a story. Darren and I had either bought them together or we all picked out ornaments on vacation. *We always bought special ornaments when we went on vacation and there was so much family history on our Christmas tree.* The truth was, I couldn't wait to take the decorations down that year. I don't like the holidays much anymore and the sooner the memories were packed away, the better. It was just too painful.

I think the second round of holidays was worse because the reality that Darren wasn't ever coming home hit me hard. This time, there were no distractions, no surgeries, neither of my kids were dating, and it was plainly just the three of us. I love my kids more than I love anything in this world and I wanted to make sure that they never felt "lonely" on the holidays. So, I over decorated, over spent, and cried, once again in silence. *Darren always so carefully and deftly wrapped the Christmas gifts in beautiful foil paper, whereas I may just be the worst present wrapper on the planet.* I miss the care he put into each gift, I miss his excitement watching us open what he thought was the perfect gift. I miss him. That second year his stocking on the mantel was a constant reminder that he wasn't home. He wasn't going to hold me; he wasn't going to have that Christmas Eve wine with me by the fire and the tree. It was just...me. No one was with me late that night when I put the presents under the tree and hoped my tears wouldn't ruin the wrapping paper. Even for the holidays, everything changed.

I have never liked New Year's Eve, what with the resolutions I could never keep and such. Darren and I would always fall asleep well before midnight. That second year; both my kids had their own plans; of which I was grateful. I, however, was alone. I watched HGTV all night and cried. I was completely alone, and sad, because everything changed so drastically for me. I talked out loud to Darren that night, begged him for forgiveness, begged for a sign, begged to be held one more time by the man who stole my heart when I was 17 years old.

I couldn't even believe it when the two year anniversary of the crash approached. I still had my game face on most of the time, I still lied and said, "I'm fine," when I was not. I missed and wanted my old life back. Yes, I had become more independent, but not by choice; it was because everything changed in my life and none of it was welcomed or wanted….none of it.

I did a news report with Jennifer West, and some of the other 3407 family members, on how 3407 friendships have evolved out of this crash. Personally, I believe no good has come out of this crash. Yes, I am friends with Jennifer, and other 3407 family members, but was that *good* that we became friends because our husbands and loved ones died? Was it *good* that legislation passed because our husbands, and others, had died? I don't think so. I will say that Jennifer is the only one in my life that truly understands how I feel. Everything changed for her too.

I got the strangest e-mail almost two and a half years after the crash. It was from a 3407 family member asking if I would participate in a meeting with Senator John Boehner, Speaker of the House, who introduced an amendment to our aviation safety bill, which was signed into law. This threatened the hard work the 3407 families fought for regarding pilot fatigue and one level of safety. The e-mail stated that the media was afraid of "me." It made me laugh but then again, it made me feel like I had accomplished 'something.' I do not want the media afraid of me. I would much rather have Colgan, Continental, and Bombardier afraid of me. I wished I did have the power to change things so badly that they would fear me, but '*I*' don't; the 3407 family group does though.

I always do my research before any interview or meeting, and this time was not different. I looked up Senator Boehner's family history and noticed that he had two daughters. I remembered thinking how lucky his girls were to have their dad. So, when I had my chance to speak, I used that researched information. I mentioned to Senator Boehner that Nikki, Summer, and nine other daughters, whose dads were on Flight 3407, would not have their fathers to tuck them in at night, hug and kiss them, or walk them down the aisle when they got married. Senator Boehner's eyes filled with tears, and I hoped that I had made a personal and emotional impact on him. I also told Senator Boehner that I had hoped he would have a safe flight back to his family. I really hoped he did. I never want another child parentless or another person without their spouse, son, daughter, brother, or sister, because a plane went down; actually, not for any reason.

I met another widow, twenty eight months after the crash. I didn't know she was a widow at first. She later told me that her husband died unexpectedly in a hunting accident. I met her at Jennifer West's house, which was even more ironic, if you ask me. Her husband had passed away nine years ago, and all I could think was, how many widows are there out there? My loss was no less or more important than her loss. It made me think; she wears her smile so well, but I know that under that smile is a heap of pain that she keeps buried deep and only lets out when "she" wants to let it out. I know this because that is what "I" do. I am so grateful I met her. She taught me about living, she reminded me not to sweat the small stuff, put life in perspective, and live the life "I" was given; without guilt. It is not that easy for me just yet.

I did not like the third holiday season without Darren either.

It was even harder than the first two for some reason. I felt

completely and utterly alone that third holiday season. Darren had

missed so much of his children's lives. I missed our daily banter,

his loud snoring, his energy, his love. I missed and miss

everything about him.

    As the third anniversary of the crash approached, everything

had changed once again. Colgan declared bankruptcy. That news

made me smile from ear to ear for days. The FAA had committed

to 1,500 hours of training for a first officer (co-pilot) in order to be

in the cockpit, as opposed to 250 hours previous. This was largely

due to the constant and continued diligence and determination of

the Flight 3407 families, a group I am honored and proud to be

associated with. We were all part of history making legislation.

Congresswoman Louise Slaughter had said that this was the

strongest aviation bill to pass AND be signed by the President in

over fifty years. I often think to myself, *I hope I made you proud*

Darren. I hope you know I did this for you, for your kids, and for everyone who buys a ticket and flies.

Three years later, my kids are doing well. I can definitely say better than me most times. They don't understand the pain that I still hide deep in my heart. August, 2011, would have been my 25th wedding anniversary, and I miss the man I fell in love with.

Darren, our son, is doing great. He graduated Summa Cum Laude from the University of Buffalo in Electrical Engineering, same as his dad. He was accepted, and was going, to Stanford for graduate school and is now working, as Electrical Engineer back home. My son runs every day and is, by all accounts, the smartest person I know. It is my hope he will meet the mother of my grandchildren soon and be blissfully happy. My son was quoted as saying, "My dad was my best friend. I had nineteen great years with my dad. Some people go a lifetime without ever having that." My son is very wise.

Nikki, where do I begin to describe our daughter? Nikki is the life and energy of our house. Her laughter is infections, her smile contagious, and her zest for life leaves me envious. She was daddy's girl; there is no doubt about that. I can't thank her friends, Casey in particular, enough for rallying around her. However, it was the kindness of one boy, Eric, that healed Nikki's broken heart, and he made my daughter happy once again. Eric and Nikki remind me a lot of my husband and I in the early dating years. We were together all the time and hated to be apart. I see so much of Darren and I in their relationship. I love that Eric brought out, once again, that contagious laugh and smile that Nikki used to wear always.

I have developed amazing friendships over the past three years. My next door neighbors, Jay and Jessica, and their three children have become like family now. I have reconnected with my childhood friends, Mary and Michele, once again. However, the most unexpected development, for me, was a unique friendship/bond I made with someone who was also hurting; the mother of Rebecca Shaw, the 1st Officer/Co-Pilot who flew

Continental Flight 3407. I reached out to Lynn Morris (Becki's mom) shortly after the crash. I wanted to let her know that I didn't hate her daughter, and I offered my sympathy. To this day, Lynn and I correspond via e-mail. We bring each other a unique strength and comfort, and I am forever grateful that I contacted her. I did try to reach out to Pilot Marvin Renslow's widow, but I was unsuccessful in contacting her.

So, how am I doing three years later? I will just say, "I'm fine," and I still wear my game face. I am, however, confident that I will learn to love the holidays once again. I am stronger now, and I am more confident in the things I do alone. Surprisingly, I no longer hate Continental, Colgan or Bombardier. I do, however, despise their actions, policies and procedures. Hate makes one ugly, it makes one bitter, and I don't want to live my life that way. I always said, "Never hate a *person*; hate their *actions*." Darren thought that was a good motto, one I shared with my students. It was time to take my own advice. I miss Darren so much, and I miss my students, and teaching, terribly too. I will always regret that I was denied the chance to visit my students and coworkers. I wanted to thank them, and tell them how they had touched *my* life. Mostly, I wanted to tell my students how proud I was of them.

Jennifer West and I have done so much together in the past three years. We had the same funeral director, and have the same attorney, financial advisors, and both our husbands worked at Northrop Grumman, so we have a lot in common. Late night texting seems to be a part of our new normal now. We both have holes in our hearts that will never be filled. I describe it as walking with a stone in your shoe; sometimes it hurts, sometimes it's just uncomfortable, but you are always aware that the stone is there. My broken and shattered heart will heal a bit, but the scar will never go away.

So what words can I offer to anyone who is grieving? First, never say "I can't." Instead say, "I am currently struggling with." Never be afraid to accept help, admit when you are weak, lean on friends and family when you need to, talk to someone in a similar situation, let go of the hate, and above all….*pray*.

My advice to everyone else is simply this: never go to bed angry at someone, do not hold grudges, tell those in your life you love them while you still can, and appreciate the blessings of family and friendships because it can be gone in an instant and everything will change.

Darren and Robin….just having fun!

In May of 2010, ten of the Flight 3407 family members got to meet the President and talk about the importance of the FAA Safety Bill getting passed. I am wearing Darren's ashes in the locket around my neck in this photo, and I made sure President Obama was aware of the significance of that locket.

(Photo: Courtesy of the White House)

Nikki and her Dad in Hawaii. Nikki was
scared and her dad promised to "never let go."

Darren (D) and Nikki outside the Congressional offices in May of 2009. They helped lobby for aviation safety in both the House and Senate, and met with the top officials of the FAA and the NTSB.
(Photo: Courtesy of Derek Gee)

This was the first time I met Jennifer and Ernie West. It was eleven days before the crash and we were at the Northrop Grumman Post Holiday Party. (Seated at the table from left to right: Jennifer West, Ernie West, Darren Tolsma, Robin Tolsma. Joe Downie, is standing above Jennifer West.)

My and Darren's wedding photo; August 29, 1986. This photo is oddly shaped because it is in a heart shaped frame and in my office at home.

Our son, Darren's, graduation from the State University of New York at Buffalo. Darren, like his father, graduated from UB Summa Cum Laude in Engineering and Applied Sciences. (Left to right: Nikki, D, and Robin)

Jennifer West and Robin Tolsma outside Senator John Brown's office after a meeting to gain his support for the FAA Safety Bill which was eventually signed into law on August 1, 2010. We carried our husband's photos everywhere in DC.

Darren, Robin, and Nikki.
My children have taught me how to smile again.

My Mom (Judy) and my Dad (Ron).

Robin and Dan Pappa.

Todd Pacer and Robin

Back row: Darren (brother), Kelley (sister-in-law)
Front row: Gwen, Lydia and Reid.

Christmas 2008; our last Christmas together.
(D, Robin, Nikki, and Darren)

Robin and Darren at the prom in 1983.
(Robin then 17, Darren was 19.)

Robin, Nikki, Congresswoman Louise
Slaughter, and D in the House Rules
Committee Chamber in Washington, DC.

Dave Hall (Navy Dave) and Robin. Dave taught me never to say, "I can't." Instead say, "I am currently struggling with…"

Ron (brother), Robin, and Darren (brother.)

Coach Kevin Carriero, beloved track coach and dear friend of Darren, Robin, D and Nikki.

Darren's urn at Forest Lawn Cemetery. The stopwatch on the right represents Darren's passion for watching his children run and the way he loved the track team.

The Flight 3407 Sarcophagus at Forest Lawn Cemetery.

Everything has changed about me, my hair, my weight, my sense of security, my new found loneliness, my continuing sadness, my heart is now broken and I have become of fighter. I want to fight for what is right, and what is fair. My husband always said, "Do the right thing, even when no one is looking." I guess it is my turn to now to be the strong one. I don't have a choice, I have to be strong, courageous, and confident, not because I wanted to, but because *everything changed.*
(Photo: Courtesy of The Buffalo News)

Left to write in the photo: John Kausner (Elly's father), Robin Tolsma (Darren's wife), Karen Wielinskin (Doug's wife), and Susan Bourque (Karen Eckert's sister).

On February 12, 2009 at 10:17 p.m., fifty one beautiful lives were lost and countless lives were forever changed. Forever in our hearts are:

Mary J. Abraham
Clarence A. Beutel II
David M. Borner
Linda L. Davidson
Ronald D. Davidson
Allison L. Des Forges
Beverly A. Eckert
Chief Master Sgt. John J. Fiore
Ronald Gonzalez
Brad S. Green Sr.
Zhaofang Guo
Ruth V. Jarel
Steven L. Johnson
Kevin W. Johnston
Georges Abu Karam
Ellyce Marie Kausner
Nicole Korczykowski and
Johnathan R. Perry
Jerome D. Krasuski
Brian David Kuklewicz
Beth Anne Kushner
Sean Andrew Lang
Madeline "Maddy" Loftus
Lorin A. Maurer
Donald McDonald

Coleman T. Mellett
Dawn M. Monachino
Dawn E. Mossop
Donald G. Mossop
Shawn M. Mossop
Jennifer E. Neil and
baby boy Neil
Gerard Joseph Niewood
Mary Belle Pettys
Donna L.Prisco
Matilda Quintero
Ferris M. Reid
Marvin Renslow
Julie Ries
John G. Roberts III
Rebecca Lynn Shaw
Dipinder Sidhu
Jean Marie Marzolf Srnecz
Darren Tolsma
Susan Alice Wehle
Ernie West
Douglas C. Wielinski
Shibin Yao
Henry Clay Yarber Jr.
Joseph Zuffoletto

Thank you Senator Charles Schumer, Congresswoman Louise Slaughter, Former Congressman Chris Lee, Congressman Brian Higgins, Senator Kristen Gillibrand, Congresswoman Kathy Hochul, and the NTSB for supporting the families of Flight 3407, and for your dedication to one level of aviation safety.

*Thank you to the following local Western New York media agencies for keeping the families of Flight 3407's goal of **one level of aviation safety** alive.*

WIVB Channel 4
WKBW Channel 7
WGRZ Channel 2
YNN Buffalo
The Buffalo News
The Bee Publications
WGRZ Radio

Lastly, thank you to the Kazmierczak family. Mom (Judy) and Dad (Ron), you have helped me through so much. You were there when I needed you and even when I didn't. Darren you were my rock for months on end. Kelley, thank you for letting Darren help me as often as he did. Kelley, you need to know you held a very special place in my husband's heart. Gwen, Lydia and Reid, you make me smile every time I see you. Ronnie, you make me laugh when I need it the most, and you let me cry, without judging me. Jennifer, Bobbi-Ann, Stephanie, and Tucker, thank you also for your support. You all stood by me, D, and Nikki. I love you all very much.

Book Extras:

To view a short clip of Darren's memorial service, please go to:
http://www.youtube.com/watch?v=ueccHmopf-g
(You can also search Youtube with the words 'Darren Tolsma 3407 Memorial')

Please feel free to check out the Families of Flight 3407 website at:
http://www.3407memorial.com/

"May you always make it home safely to your loved ones. Godspeed"

~Robin Tolsma

Made in the USA
Lexington, KY
18 May 2012